Original title:
Green Pastures of Poetry

Copyright © 2025 Creative Arts Management OÜ
All rights reserved.

Author: Rosalie Bradford
ISBN HARDBACK: 978-1-80567-078-0
ISBN PAPERBACK: 978-1-80567-158-9

Verses Dancing on Windswept Hills

On a hill where daisies spin,
And breezes dare to declare a win,
A line tripped over its own rhyme,
And chuckled at its silly crime.

The daisies giggled, swayed with flair,
As poets chased their dreams in air,
But one fell flat, in mud it landed,
And all the other verses banded.

A squirrel critiqued their poetic grace,
While scribbling notes in a hurried pace,
"You need some humor, that's the key!"
And danced away on a shard of glee.

Serenity in the Wildflower Pages

In the meadow, where bluebells sway,
A poem sneezed and blew away,
It tickled the petals, oh what a sight,
As laughter echoed throughout the night.

The wildflowers wore hats with pride,
As verses hopped on a bumpy ride,
With bees buzzing out epic tunes,
And butterflies prancing like silly loons.

A daffodil dared to do the twist,
While the shy violets just couldn't resist,
They giggled and twirled, daring the sun,
Creating a scene like no other fun.

The Canvassed Corners of Thought

In corners where bright ideas bloom,
A thought rolled out, no hints of gloom,
It tickled the canvas with vibrant hues,
And danced on the page, slipped on its shoes.

A painter joined with a giggly brush,
Creating a scene that made us hush,
But then the paint took a trip too far,
And splattered laughter, our new bizarre.

With each brushstroke, a chuckle grew,
As everyone laughed, they knew what to do,
They splashed out verses in colors bold,
Creating stories that never grow old.

Rhythms of Rustling Reeds

By the lake, reeds rustle in song,
Each note a quirk, where all belong,
A frog croaked loud, a clumsy try,
And other critters joined with a sigh.

The tadpoles twisted in sheer delight,
As verses jived into the night,
A turtle tapped its shell in beat,
Creating rhythms that shook each seat.

But a breeze swept in with a lively tease,
The chorus sang, aimed to please,
As laughter rippled across the pond,
In nudges and giggles, beyond and beyond.

The Bounty of Unwritten Tales

In fields of ink, the thoughts run free,
With cows that rhyme and bushes that decree.
A tree that jokes, with branches that sway,
And butterflies chatting, brightening the day.

If only the pen could spill its delight,
As rabbits recite limericks in flight.
The grass tickles toes, a playful invite,
To dance with ideas that frolic all night.

Lush Landscapes of the Mind's Eye.

In a valley where giggles grow wild and loud,
The daisies wear hats, quite joyous and proud.
Silly squirrels scribble their letters askew,
While the sun gives a wink, its warmth breaking through.

A pond filled with puns, it splashes with glee,
As frogs recite sonnets, oh so poetically.
Each ripple a chuckle, a chorus so bright,
Painting visions that shimmer, pure silly delight.

Whispers of Emerald Meadows

In meadows where laughter is soft as a brook,
The daisies debate which way to look.
A hedgehog pens letters with a tip of its quill,
While ladybugs giggle at the thrill of the spill.

A breeze brings the news, wrapped in a rhyme,
Of chickens that copy the catwalk in time.
With every soft whisper, the flowers all sway,
Tickling each other in a humorous play.

Beneath the Canopy of Verses

Beneath branches scribbling in playful delight,
A parrot regales with tales through the night.
An owl drops the beat, as the verses take flight,
While mice in their suits keep the rhythm just right.

With acorns that giggle and leaves made of rhyme,
Each creature creates a new world on a dime.
In this lively haven, where humor sings bright,
The canopy holds every pun meant to light.

The Sonnet of Swaying Grasses

In fields where tall grasses dance with glee,
The cows have started joining in the sway.
A goat named Fred dons shades, looks fancy—
While chickens herd by, cock-a-doodle all day.

Beneath a tree, a poet takes a seat,
His muse is munching snacks, what a delight!
He writes of cows that tap dance on their feet,
And just then, they start a cow-jazz night!

Lush Verses in Nature's Embrace

The trees gossip high, with rustling leaves,
As squirrels try to steal their wooden words.
The flowers giggle, making humorous heaves,
While bees recite rhymes like little nerds.

A frog wearing glasses croaks poetry fine,
His voice is a croak, like a broken bell.
The dandelions think they're quite divine,
While ants recite sonnets, do tell!

The Garden of Stanzas and Dreams

In a garden alive with rhymes and jest,
The carrots wear hats, quite a posh affair.
Tomatoes play tag, doing their best,
While radishes grumble, but who really cares?

Sunflowers tilt to hear the jokes in bloom,
With petals like ears, they nod and sway.
A butterfly burst in giggles, no gloom,
As nature's comedians play every day!

Fields of Rhyme and Reflection

In fields where poetry grows like weeds,
The cows try to rhyme but just moo instead.
A sheep with a pencil is jotting down creeds,
While pigs share a story that's just in their head.

The wind whispers lines, but they all sound crude,
As ducks quack in rhythm, a splashing beat.
The breeze joins in, feeling very rude,
Tickling all, has nature skipped a beat?

Wandering through the Written Wilds

In a field of rhymes I stroll,
Chasing verses, what a goal!
Butterflies write on the breeze,
While I chase them, oh, if you please.

The trees giggle with leafy quips,
And the flowers dance with colorful tips.
Napping bees hum strange old tunes,
While I decipher their buzzing secrets by the moon.

Each step I take makes the ink spill,
The grass tickles my feet, what a thrill!
The mushrooms whisper silly jokes,
And the daisies laugh at clumsy folks.

In this wild, they call me scribe,
Plucking words, like bees from a hive.
But losing my pen in the thicket,
Hoping my thoughts won't end up as a cricket!

Paths Carved in Nature's Ink

Through tangled words, I wander free,
Where the trees retell tales of me.
The bark's not dry, it's full of sass,
Whispering stories of the past.

Down the path of prose I trot,
A rhyme here, a giggle, it's quite a lot!
Frogs croak sonnets in perfect tune,
As I dance around, a poetic buffoon.

Leaves in hand, snippets of cheer,
Can I wear them? Well, oh dear!
The wind laughs and bows to my plight,
As I trip over roots, oh what a sight!

Caught in nature's inexplicable sway,
Every daffodil composes a play.
This forest is where humor sprouts,
As I pen lines amidst nature's shouts!

The Ethereal Voice of Greenery

Whispers of leaves, a giggle or two,
They teach me how to write and chew.
Squirrels recite lines with nuts in hand,
While I marvel at their poetic band.

A rose cracked a joke about a thorn,
And daisies debated who'd be reborn.
Every branch sways in comedic glee,
As nature sits back and laughs at me.

In this vibrant realm, there's no dread,
Just echoes of laughter, nowhere to tread.
With every stanza, I trip and fall,
And the daisies snicker at it all!

Though I scribble with joy, my pen takes flight,
A firefly spins tales into the night.
In this greenery, fun grows tall,
And laughter is what I hear most of all!

Mosaic of Words in Nature's Bower

Within this bower, words collide,
Poems ripple like water, wide!
Twigs are the pens, the grass holds ink,
As I gather giggles more than I think.

A chipmunk declares today's news,
While a hedgehog dons metallic shoes.
Laughter floats on the currant breeze,
And fuzzy flowers sway with ease.

In this colorful patch, phrases twist,
As the sun creates a warmth-filled mist.
My pen's a wand, casting spells profound,
Bringing forth chuckles from the ground.

With every step, the earth gives cheer,
Leaves scribble in a language clear.
In this comical crowd where I reside,
Even jackrabbits take poetic pride!

The Flourish of Untamed Lyrics

In a field where verses grow,
Limericks dance to and fro.
Jokes are scattered like seeds,
Sprouting laughter, yes, indeed!

Puns pop up from every side,
As rhymes take off for a ride.
Slogans flutter on the breeze,
Wrapped in humor, just like cheese!

Each line a whimsical treat,
A sonnet with two left feet.
As verses tumble with grace,
Words pirouette, what a race!

In this garden of delight,
We find joy in every write.
So come join this merry spree,
Where laughter flows wild and free!

Wandering Through Wordy Meadows

In meadows of chatter and cheer,
Words skip and play, never fear.
With metaphors jumping around,
And similes tumbling down!

I tripped on a rhyme so grand,
It offered me a helping hand.
Said, "Don't just stand there, be bold!"
So I danced with tales untold.

Butterflies flaunt puns in flight,
Tickling all with sheer delight.
Each step a verse, light and fun,
Count the giggles, we've just begun!

Let's frolic in lines that amaze,
And laugh through these silly phase.
With every twist, a new surprise,
In these meadows, joy never dies!

Vibrant Stems of Rhyme

Bouncing bulbs of cleverness sprout,
Each line a chuckle, there's no doubt.
With a wink and a quirky jest,
These verses are truly the best!

Petals flutter in giggly breeze,
While birds whistle rhymes with such ease.
A daffodil told me a pun,
Now I laugh till the day is done!

Tulips sway in hilarious fits,
Joking 'bout poems and knitting mitts.
With every stem, a joke unfurls,
In this land, whimsy twirls and whirls!

So let's gather these rhymes so bright,
And share them in jovial light.
For humor's the root we embrace,
In this flowery, joyous space!

The Whispering Willows of Reflection

Beneath the willows where shadows play,
Whispers of chuckles float our way.
With every rustle, a giggly sound,
Where humor's treasures abound!

Swaying branches tell funny tales,
Of mishaps and friend's epic fails.
Echoes of laughter fill the air,
As silly thoughts dance everywhere!

Reflecting on life with a grin,
Finding joy where we've been.
With a quip or a witticism right,
We'll chuckle till the stars ignite!

So settle down, let laughter spring,
In the shade where jokers sing.
With every word, a light-hearted cheer,
In whispering willows, we have no fear!

The Treasure of the Blossoming Script

In fields where phrases play so bright,
The daisies write by morning light.
With giggles swirling in the breeze,
They dance and rhyme among the trees.

A squirrel drafts a silly verse,
While rabbits hop, rehearsing worse.
Each word is sprinkled with delight,
As characters take flight at night.

The flowers have opinions too,
They bloom in colors, quite uncouth.
A rose proclaims, 'I'm best of all!'
While lilacs laugh and have a ball.

We pause and share a hearty chuckle,
As every line's a jolly buckle.
In this wild realm of written cheer,
We find the treasure of good cheer.

Strokes of Light on Written Green

With every stroke, the canvas glows,
As sunlight giggles and gently flows.
The pen transforms the grass to prose,
A waltz of ink where humor grows.

Chirping birds provide the score,
Their tweets a quirk, we can't ignore.
They tease and chirp, their verses fly,
As butterflies all wink and sigh.

A rabbit plots a tale of cheese,
While sneaky ants perform with ease.
Their stories twist like vines of fun,
Where shadows play and sunbeams run.

In every stroke, a laugh appears,
As nature whispers in our ears.
Each written word, a joyful spree,
In this bright realm of poetry.

Voice of the Wind Through the Foliage

The wind, it chuckles through the leaves,
   It carries tales that tease and weave.
   A breeze that tickles laughter's soul,
   And every branch becomes a scroll.

   Amidst the rustle, stories swell,
   Of silly squirrels and misty spells.
   They run about, each tale they spin,
   With leaves all clapping, let's begin!

   A wind that howls in goofy tones,
Makes whispers dance on boughs and stones.
   As moles compose a concert grand,
   With beats that ripple through the land.

   In every gust, a giggle's found,
   As nature jokes swirl all around.
   So listen close to winds that play,
   For laughter waits at every sway.

Nature's Poetry Woven in Time

In the fabric of the earth's delight,
Where petals chat and fungi light.
A patchwork quilt of laughter spun,
With threads of jokes and endless fun.

The brook, it bubbles, sharing glee,
Each ripple sings a melody.
The stones join in with smirks galore,
As nature's voice, we can't ignore.

A dandelion thinks it's the king,
With wishes tossed on winds that sing.
While crickets chirp their slyest schemes,
We laugh at all our leafy dreams.

In every nook, a poem flows,
With whimsy sweet, as laughter grows.
So let us dance on rhymes divine,
In this bright tapestry of time.

The Rooted Cadence of Scenes

In fields of rhyme, cows play chess,
A goat in glasses, feeling blessed.
Beneath the sun, pigs dance a jig,
As roosters rap, it's quite a gig.

The daisies clap, they cheer and sway,
While bunnies plot their next ballet.
The breeze hums tunes, a silly song,
With every note, nothing can go wrong.

An owl in trousers, what a sight,
Navigates the day, denies the night.
A donkey jesters with words so sly,
While butterflies flaunt, oh my, oh my!

So gather near, let's share a laugh,
In this wild world of silly gaffs.
Where laughter grows amid the green,
And every moment's a joyous scene.

Fables in the Shade of Trees

Under the boughs where stories dwell,
A squirrel reads, and does it well.
Beneath a shade, the foxes scheme,
While turtles dream a racing dream.

With every tale, the acorns laugh,
As robins sing of a silly gaffe.
The woodpecker drums a funky beat,
While ants march by on sticky feet.

A wise old crow spins tales of yore,
Of frogs in tuxedos by the door.
And in the shade, the laughter rings,
As crickets chirp, 'long live the kings!'

So let us pause, our worries cease,
For in this shade, we find our peace.
Where fables rhyme and joy is free,
In the heart of nature's jubilee.

Blossoms of Imagination Awakened

In gardens bright where dreams take flight,
A sunflower dons a tutu, what a sight!
The daisies giggle, twirling round,
While tulip trumpets sound off loud.

Oh, bumblebees in suits parade,
Chatting of nectar and lemonade.
The roses plot a theater show,
As daisies audition, putting on a glow.

With each new bloom, a tale begins,
Of mice that wear oversized fins.
They swim through air, it's quite absurd,
In a world where silly's never blurred.

So wander here, let laughter gleam,
Among the petals of a dream.
For in these blooms, imagination thrives,
And every whim, oh how it jives!

Streams of Thought in Blooming Fields

In meadows wide where thoughts run free,
A sheep recites a philosophy.
The daisies nod with wise insight,
While frogs debate the meaning of light.

A river flows with puns galore,
As fish tell jokes that start a roar.
The willow bends, it laughs so light,
While daisies dance to the day's delight.

With every ripple, laughter spreads,
As crickets weave their webs in threads.
The sun dips low with a silly grin,
As night begins, let fun begin!

So join the flow, let worries cease,
In this realm of laughter and peace.
Where streams of thought like giggles blend,
And every whim finds a joyful end.

Lines of Love Amidst the Lilies

In the garden of giggles, we sing,
Plucking rhymes like daisies each spring.
Bumblebees buzz with their own little tune,
While we chase shadows beneath the bright moon.

Ticklish thoughts dance on the breeze,
Haikus float by, rustling the leaves.
With every line, a chuckle will grow,
In this floral farce, we steal the show.

A sonnet slips on a banana peel,
Limericks laugh, oh, what a deal!
The poet's heart, it jumps and twirls,
Sprinkling joy in lyrical swirls.

Every petal has a punchline, it seems,
Giggles and grins fuel our dreams.
In this field of silly, we shall remain,
Crafting our verses, a joyous refrain.

A Dance of Ink Under the Sun

The ink spills like juice from a fruit,
Dancing around in a wild pursuit.
With every splash, a story we weave,
The sun giggles, it can hardly believe.

Quills twirl like couples at a ball,
Scribbles wobble, do not fear the fall.
A paper plane takes off in delight,
Soaring on winds of mischief and light.

Sunshine tickles the edge of the page,
Laughing at poems that break from their cage.
With each dot and line, a grin appears,
Spreading like laughter, carried by cheers.

Silliness sprinkles like confetti bright,
Each stanza a spark in the warm sunlight.
A dance of ink, let it never be done,
For words are a party, a whip-smart pun!

The Enclave of Quiet Reflection

In a corner where thoughts like to nap,
Whispers of wisdom form quite a map.
Silly musings in cozy arrays,
Nestled together like warm sunny rays.

Pondering what might a cactus say,
If given the chance to joke and play.
A laugh here, a giggle there so sweet,
As we sit on cushions, taking a seat.

Grinning quietly at a bemused cat,
Who plots a course for a nap, imagine that!
With every sigh, some giggles will rise,
As we nibble on dreams, what a surprise!

The enclave hums with laughter so bright,
The echoes of joy bouncing in daylight.
Here, we discover in soft contemplation,
The essence of humor is pure elation.

The Rapture of Alive Verses

Verses awaken with a gleeful cheer,
Dancing on pages, bringing us near.
Each word a tickle, a playful embrace,
Inviting us into their joyful space.

The rhymes are merry, like children at play,
Swinging on swings, as they shout hooray!
Every line bursts with laughter's own sound,
In this rapture of joy, we're blissfully bound.

A metaphor trips and falls to a knee,
While similes giggle with innocent glee.
In the garden of lines where silliness grows,
Let your laughter flow, let your joy overflow.

Alive with the rhythm, we skip and we hop,
With poetry's joy, we'll never stop.
So gather your words, let them dance and swirl,
In this rapture of verses, let laughter unfurl.

Garden of Thoughts in Full Bloom

In the garden of dreams, I trip on my feet,
Picking daisies of wisdom, so wondrously sweet.
Butterflies gossip, they flutter and fly,
While I chase my thoughts like a cat with a pie.

We plant seeds of laughter, the weeds grow tall,
I wonder if they'll show up to the ball.
Rainclouds above have a party tonight,
While I dance in my socks, feeling quite light.

A gopher offers me a slice of his cheese,
I tap my toe to the rhythm of trees.
In this wacky garden, I bake jokes in the sun,
And if laughter is cake, then I've already won.

The tulips all chuckle, with petals so bright,
While squirrels make banners, all ready for flight.
So come join the fun, there's enough to go 'round,
In this garden of thoughts, happiness abounds.

The Harmony of Earth and Ink

With pencils and plants, we'll sketch out a tune,
Make verses in soil, beneath a bright moon.
The worms join the chorus, they wiggle their lore,
While the daisies chime in, then fall to the floor.

My journal's a picnic, it spreads on the grass,
With crumbs of ideas, they tumble and pass.
I spill ink on the beetles, they dance with a grin,
A scribble of laughter, let the fun begin.

Puns blossom like flowers, so silly and bold,
Each one a secret that needs to be told.
The toads hold a concert, croaking in style,
As the sun sets in colors that make us all smile.

So grab a good rhyming, let verses ignite,
In the harmony found where the earth meets the light.
In a garden of stories, where ink flows like streams,
We'll craft all our laughter, our very best dreams.

Meadows of Metaphor and Muse

In a meadow of metaphors, the cows wear hats,
They skip and they prance, all chubby and fat.
The flowers are pondering absurd little schemes,
While I'm in the background, lost in my dreams.

A butterfly whispers, "What's the joke today?"
"I'm late for my breakfast!" the rooster will bray.
I tickle the daisies, they giggle and sway,
As I write down these thoughts that seem to outrun play.

A bumblebee buzzes, "Hey, don't forget me!"
"I'll join you in verse, we'll form quite the spree!"
So together we frolic through sunlight and shade,
In a meadow of muses, where laughter won't fade.

The grass sends me puns, I carefully weave,
As clouds doodle rainbows, oh, how they believe!
In this whimsical world where silliness rules,
We'll create a delight that's beyond all the schools.

Lyrical Landscapes of the Heart

In landscapes of laughter, my heart takes a stroll,
With marshmallow mountains that playfully roll.
I trip over punchlines, they tumble so fine,
While the rivers of rhythm hum sweetly in line.

A hedgehog recites, with a twinkle of glee,
"Life's best when it's quirky, come laugh here with me!"
The foliage flutters, it adds to the cheer,
As the saplings jump up, shouting, "We're here!"

With quips like the sunbeams that glitter and shine,
A sunfish serenades, "Oh, won't you be mine?"
Through valleys of giggles and hills made of jest,
We'll plant seeds of joy and let humor invest.

So join in this journey, so wild and absurd,
Where the heart finds its rhythm through laughter and word.
In these lyrical lands, we'll dance in delight,
Creating a poem from dusk until night.

Where Inspiration Flourishes Abundantly

In fields of words, the ideas dance,
A gust of thoughts, a fleeting chance.
With dandelions sprouting rhymes,
I scribble down the silliest crimes.

The sunbeams tease the timid bees,
While squirrels plot their perfect tease.
Rabbits hop with glee untold,
In this realm, magic unfolds.

A crow caws jokes above my head,
As clouds above my notebook spread.
I chase the gags, I chase the gleam,
Filling pages, a joy-filled dream.

Oh muse of mischief, come on through,
Let's spin some tales, both strange and new.
In laughter's grip, I make my stand,
In this bright land, all's wonderfully planned.

The Untamed Rhyme of Flora

Petals giggle as they bloom,
With laughter wafting from each room.
A tulip tickles every bee,
While laughing lice climb up a tree.

The daisies tell their silly jokes,
And tease the prudent, proper folks.
In every stem, a story's found,
While giggly roots frolic underground.

The violets wear their purple crowns,
While daisies pull their petals down.
In this garden, nonsense grows,
With every leaf, a punchline shows.

Oh nature's fun, a vibrant sight,
Where every garden bursts with light.
With blooms that babble, life's a jest,
In this wild patch, we're truly blessed.

Nature's Quill etches Rhythmic Tales

With feathered pen, the wind takes flight,
And scribbles laughter day and night.
The leaves recite their leafy lore,
While critters play upon the floor.

In whispers soft, the grass conveys,
A symphony of funny ways.
The squirrel writes a slapstick play,
As sunlight dances on the day.

A brook chuckles, bubbling bright,
While frogs croak rhymes, a sheer delight.
Each ripple sings a goofy tune,
Beneath the watchful, grinning moon.

So gather round, hear nature's cheer,
With quills of joy, let's draw them near.
In every tale, let laughter reign,
In this bright world, we'll keep it sane.

The Radiance of Earth's Poetry

Beneath the skies, the verses weave,
With ticklish winds that laugh and cleave.
In sunlit fields, the grass does sway,
Creating rhymes in a playful way.

The flowers giggle, painted bright,
In colors bold, a comical sight.
With every bee and buzzing sound,
The laws of humor here abound.

Oh, dancing clouds with playful grace,
Bring whimsy to this open space.
The chirping birds compose the tunes,
Of jovial tales beneath the moons.

So join the dance, let words take flight,
In this realm where all feels right.
With every line, we laugh and grin,
In the heart of earth, the fun begins.

Whispers of the Verdant Muse

In the meadow where words play,
Unicorns dance, oh what a display!
Ideas sprout from the ground,
In each giggle, a thought is found.

Silly squirrels write rhymes with glee,
Chasing rabbits, wild and free.
Puns grow like daisies in the sun,
Making every line a funny pun.

Strolling poets trip on their feet,
With laughter echoing, oh what a treat!
Butterflies join in the fun,
As verses flutter, one by one.

Breezes carry the jests afar,
While frogs croak in their own bizarre.
In this field of whimsy so bright,
Every quip feels just right.

Fields of Imagination's Bloom

A chicken struts with saucy flair,
Clucks a sonnet without a care.
The daffodils join, they sing loud,
Promising laughter to the crowd.

A dandelion, all puffy and grand,
Whispers secrets of the land.
Bumblebees buzz with comic grace,
Stealing nectar from every place.

The trees start giggling, can't keep still,
As pinecones tumble down the hill.
Clouds roll by with a wink and a nudge,
Tickling the earth, giving a smudge.

In this spot, where silliness thrums,
Even the squirrels can't keep mum.
Words sprout like weeds without a fight,
In a garden where laughter feels right.

The Lush Symphony of Words

The trumpet of a toad croaks out a tune,
While flowers wiggle beneath the moon.
Each stanza hops with playful cheer,
Drawing in critters from far and near.

A concert led by the wind so spry,
Leaves rustling in a soft sigh.
Hiccups of laughter fill the air,
As poets join in without a care.

Caterpillars in their cozy waits,
Spin their verses while munching on dates.
Ants march in rhythm, a parade of jest,
Finding humor is always the best.

In this symphony of leaf and sound,
Joyous rhymes can always be found.
So let every creature shake and sway,
As we dance in the words we play.

Tapestry of Nature's Verses

Weaving words on a grassy loom,
A tapestry brightens the gloomiest room.
Butterflies stitch with colorful thread,
While jammy bees buzz overhead.

The daisies entertain with a twist,
Throwing a party that none can resist.
They giggle and whisper, twist and twirl,
As poets gladly give it a whirl.

A gentle breeze carries the banter on high,
While crickets chirp under the starry sky.
Each line a, tickle, each verse a hug,
Unraveled laughter in this cozy snug.

In this land of whimsy, joy does reside,
As all of nature joins in with pride.
So come, take part in this merriment grand,
With verses and laughter, we'll make our stand.

Emerald Dreams Beneath the Sky

In fields where poets tread so light,
The grass is tall, the sun is bright.
They scribble lines, a bit askew,
While rabbits giggle, 'Who are you?'

A twist of fate, a rhyme misplaced,
The parrot squawks, "You've lost your grace!"
A limerick bounces like a ball,
As clouds above begin to sprawl.

They write of love and silly things,
Of cats in hats and birds with bling.
Yet laughter bubbles, spilling free,
As nature joins their poetry.

So if you find a sunny patch,
Where words and giggles seem to hatch,
Join in the fun, don't be so shy,
In dreams of emerald, we all fly!

Where The Wild Stanzas Grow

In a meadow where the verses sprout,
A stanza dances, leaping about.
It twirls with grass and jumps on rocks,
While ants debate the rhyme in socks.

A quirky squirrel, with a feather pen,
Writes of acorns and mischievous men.
The flowers shout, "Oh what a sight!"
As bees compose their buzz in flight.

With each new line, a giggle grows,
The wind plays tricks, and laughter flows.
Poetry's wild, a laughing spree,
Where all the rhymes sip herbal tea.

So wander here, where rhythm's free,
Let nonsense flow like honey bee.
In this patch of verse, life is a show,
Where every giggle helps it grow!

Chasing Leaves of Lyricism

In swirling winds, the words take flight,
Like autumn leaves, a comical sight.
They twirl and dance, both bold and free,
While turtles contemplate their spree.

A frog jumps up with a silly croak,
He stirs the lines, causing a joke.
The whispering trees join in the cheer,
"Catch that leaf! It's coming near!"

Chasing lines through a poetic maze,
The squirrels applaud the playful phrase.
With laughter bending every branch,
They take a turn, and now they dance.

So let your heart sing with the breeze,
And tickle the clouds with gentle ease.
For in this chase of bold ideas,
You'll find the joy amidst your fears!

Sunlit Canopy of Expression

Beneath the sun, where shadows play,
A poet lounges the day away.
With humor stacked like playful bricks,
He jots down lines, sharing his tricks.

Among the branches, laughter rings,
The fruit trees boast of silly things.
A bird with style, a fancy dress,
Twirls in rhyme, adorned with fest.

The breeze whispers tales of the day,
In twisted lines that seem to sway.
With every giggle, every cheer,
The world becomes a stage right here.

So raise a glass to sunlit glee,
Where every verse feels wild and free.
Join in the fun, let laughter spread,
In this bright canopy, joy is bred!

The Fragrance of Words in Bloom

In the garden of phrases, words start to play,
They twist and they turn in a comical way,
With giggles of grammar, they tumble and spin,
Like bees on a mission, they buzz and they grin.

Puns blossom like flowers, all colorful, bright,
Each chuckle a petal, a pure delight,
They dance on the winds, a whimsical toast,
To laughter that blooms, we celebrate most.

Metaphors sprout, with a quirk and a twist,
Giving rhymes a new coat, oh, how can we resist?
Each sonnet a seed, oh, how it will glow,
In the sunlight of laughter, we'll let the words flow.

So gather your verses, under sky so wide,
The fragrance of laughter, let's cherish with pride,
In the fields of expression, where humor grows free,
We'll celebrate joy, just you wait and see!

Verses Cascading Like Gentle Rain

Words flutter like raindrops, dropping from above,
Dancing on the pages, a rhythm to love,
Each line like a puddle, where laughter can splash,
A cascade of chuckles, a humorous dash.

With quips as the droplets, they sprinkle with cheer,
Like ducks in a row, they quack without fear,
Each stanza a river, that flows with such glee,
Witty as a weasel, as sharp as can be.

Like showers of glimmers, they giggle and glide,
Creating a rainbow with words as the guide,
The verses keep flowing, like water so sweet,
Come dance in the rain, and feel the heart beat.

In this pool of puns, we splash and dive deep,
Where laughter's the secret we happily keep,
So let's sing of the sizzle, of words in refrain,
In the merriment garden, let's frolic and gain!

The Heart's Harvest in the Field of Words

In a field full of verses, we gather them bright,
With baskets of punchlines, what a glorious sight!
Each joke is a fruit, ripe for the picking,
Their sweetness invites us, and laughter keeps kicking.

With rhymes like tomatoes, and puns like peas,
Our harvest of humor flows gracefully with ease,
We'll munch on the verses, oh how they will fill,
And savor the flavors that tickle and thrill.

Let's plant seeds of insight among jokes and jest,
Where puns pop like popcorn and never do rest,
We'll celebrate the banquet of wit that we share,
In this whimsical garden, with love in the air.

So join in the laughter, let's fill up our hearts,
The bounty of humor, let's share its fine arts,
In this fertile patch where the funny things bloom,
Together we'll giggle, let's make the leap zoom!

Resonance of the Flora and Fauna

In a patch of pure laughter, the critters all play,
The words are the flowers that brighten the day,
With squirrels who chatter and birds that croon,
Each quirk in the air makes the whole forest swoon.

The bees are the poets, they buzz with delight,
While worms tell their tales from morning till night,
The trees whisper secrets, their branches do sway,
In this raucous garden, let's frolic and play.

Fragrance of humor wafts up in the breeze,
Like daisies in laughter, they dance with such ease,
With quips sprouting fast like a vine in full bloom,
The giggles keep rising, they chase out the gloom.

So join in the revelry, let nature rejoice,
With each chuckle and giggle, give laughter a voice,
In this land of imagination, so vast and alive,
The resonance of whimsy will help us to thrive!

Canvases of Clover and Rhyme

In fields where daisies dance with glee,
A beetle sings a tune, oh me!
With crayons made of sunshine bright,
We scribble verses, pure delight.

The grass grows tall, it looks like hair,
A sheep leaps high, without a care.
It chews on rhymes like tasty treats,
And hops around on little feet.

Our pens are ducks that quack and croon,
They flutter by and steal the moon.
Each line we write brings giggles loud,
A funny place, we're all so proud.

So grab your hats, your boots, your socks,
Let's write some lines before the clocks!
In clover fields, our laughter's free,
Creating joy as wild as can be.

The Sprout of Creative Harvest

From seeds of thought, our words do grow,
In silly shapes, they dance and flow.
A tomato tells a joke so sly,
While carrots grin as time goes by.

We gather rhymes like fruits at noon,
A melon winks—it's quite a boon!
Jokes tumble out like peas from pods,
We giggle loud and nod at odds.

With every line, our smiles bloom bright,
A patch of joy, it feels so right.
Let's plant our dreams in rows so neat,
A harvest strange, but oh-so-sweet!

So grab a scythe, let's cut some fun,
In fields of laughter, we all run.
Creativity's in every sprout,
In playful jest, we twist and shout.

Kaleidoscope of Rejuvenating Lines

In swirling colors, verses spin,
With laughter loud, the fun begins.
A rainbow writes its own delight,
Each word a wink, a giggle light.

The sky's our canvas, never stark,
A polka dot brings forth a spark.
As butterflies compose in flight,
They write their tales, a pure delight.

With every line, a twist and twirl,
A jester's hat begins to whirl.
We dance on words like sprightly dews,
And harvest joy with silly views.

So let's create a playful mix,
A jigsaw made of wordy tricks.
The colors blend, we laugh and cheer,
In this wild land, there's naught to fear.

Serenity in Leafy Sonnets

Beneath the trees, the whispers play,
A squirrel thinks he's Shakespeare, hey!
With acorns acting as his props,
He spins his tales, the laughter hops.

The leaves compose a gentle tune,
While crickets chirp beneath the moon.
A fox writes sonnets in the night,
And shares his tales with pure delight.

The grasshoppers join in the fun,
With leaps so high, their work is done.
In leafy realms, we find our grace,
With every line, a laughing space.

So gather 'round, let rhymes take flight,
In nature's arms, our hearts feel light.
The sonnets sway, they never tire,
In leafy realms, we spark the fire.

Stanzas Beneath the Shade of Oaks

Under branches wide and bright,
A squirrel dances, what a sight!
With acorns flying here and there,
I duck and dodge, oh where's my hair?

The grass tickles my toes so fine,
As ants parade in single line,
They march with purpose, heads held high,
While I just lie and let out a sigh.

A bird above begins to squawk,
Suggesting lunch? Oh, do come talk!
But all it does is call for cheer,
While I still ponder my next beer.

So join me in this shaded scene,
Where life is silly, yet so serene,
For under oaks, with friends nearby,
We laugh and joke 'til time slips by.

A Symphony of Verdant Lyrics

The grass is singing, can you hear?
While leaves perform a jig, my dear,
A caterpillar joins the show,
While flowers sway to and fro.

The breeze is like a winking tease,
It rustles leaves with giggles, please!
A chorus of frogs begins to croak,
As if they tell the world's best joke.

Bees buzz in tunes, a busy band,
While daisies sway—they're all quite grand,
They nod their heads with every beat,
While ants keep dancing on their feet.

So grab a seat upon the grass,
Let nature's concert come to pass,
With laughter blooming everywhere,
This symphony delights the air!

The Tapestry of Nature's Ballad

In fields adorned with golden hue,
There's a tale weaving 'round for you,
A rabbit hops, with ears so long,
It sings to crows a silly song.

The daisies giggle in a row,
While butterflies put on a show,
They flutter by with painted wings,
As if to mock our serious things.

A breeze turns whispers into jest,
As flowers lean in for a rest,
They share their secrets, bloom by bloom,
While bees just buzz in total gloom.

With laughter sprouting everywhere,
This tapestry holds joy to share,
So join the fun, don't miss your chance,
To twirl and skip in nature's dance!

Sonorous Trails of Burbling Brooks

A brook babbles tales of great delight,
As pebbles laugh, reflecting light,
They splash and dance, a merry crew,
While frogs croak out their morning view.

The fish dive down for secret plans,
While crickets form their little bands,
They chirp with glee, a quirky tune,
That makes the sun shine brighter soon.

A family of ducks starts to waddle,
With little ones in playful dawdle,
They quack in rhythm, what a sight,
As I can't help but laugh outright.

So pause a moment, take a look,
At nature's page, like open book,
With burbling trails and silly cheer,
Come join the fun, the end is near!

Where the Wild Words Grow

In the land of scribbles, words run free,
Chasing their tails like a bumblebee.
They giggle and tumble, a merry old sight,
Dancing on pages in pure delight.

Puns sprout like daisies, colorful and bright,
Tickling your funny bone, what a delight!
Rhyme schemes race like rabbits on the run,
In this quirky garden, laughter's never done.

The similes stretch like a cat in the sun,
Imagery so vivid, it's all in good fun.
Metaphors grow tall, like a tree in the sky,
With branches of nonsense, they wave goodbye.

Here, inspiration's always a good friend,
A jester dressed in leaves, it'll never end.
So come with your pens and let's have a blast,
In this wild wonderland, we'll make stories last.

Echoes Among the Leafy Lines

In the forest of verses, whispers go 'boo',
Words play hide and seek, just like me and you.
Each leaf a letter, each branch a new rhyme,
Together they giggle, having a good time.

The squirrels hold meetings, debating their prose,
While owls in the branches cheer with a pose.
They scratch their furry heads over a joke,
While a nearby fox chuckles, giving a poke.

Laughter echoes softly, a sweet serenade,
In this leafy arena, no thoughts ever fade.
Nature's a chorus, singing out loud,
While pitter-patter rain joins as a crowd.

So if you hear giggles among the tall trees,
Know that the verses float onward with ease.
Join in the fun, let your humor take flight,
In this lively jungle, everything feels right.

Ink and the Blossoming Landscape

Ink droplets fall like rain from the sky,
Splash on the paper, oh my, oh my!
With every splash, a story is born,
Crafted with giggles, and nobody's sworn.

Pencils turn into flowers that bloom,
Sending out fragrances, dispelling the gloom.
They twirl and they twist, in a poetic ballet,
Creating new shenanigans in their own way.

Colors of humor paint the horizon bright,
As verses come to life, what a comical sight!
With every line drawn, a new chuckle grows,
In this boundless field where silliness flows.

So let us frolic in this ink-painted land,
Where every word's a pet, in a mischievous band.
With laughter in our hearts as we scribble and play,
This landscape of joy will never decay.

The Poetry of Sunlit Glades

In the sunlit glades where the laughter's sweet,
Words do a jig, tapping their feet.
Each stanza bounces with bounce and flair,
Tickling the sunbeams dancing in air.

Grasshoppers join in with a jaunt and a leap,
As verses tumble out, no need for sleep.
Fireflies wink, with a mischievous glow,
While giggles and rumbles make the humor flow.

Syllables twist and shout like at a fair,
While the butterflies giggle without a care.
They flutter around, adding sparkle and cheer,
In this bright place, joy is always near.

So come take a stroll through these playful lines,
Where every word bops and brightly shines.
In the warmth of the sun, let's write some more,
In this enchanting glade, laughter's never a chore.

Heartstrings Tied to the Roots of Rhyme

In the garden, my heart is wooed,
With verses sprouting, never subdued.
The daisies giggle as I recite,
They tease me back in the morning light.

Crickets songwrite, I can't keep pace,
Chasing syllables all over the place.
A butterfly winks, says 'What's the fuss?'
While I trip over my own rhyming bus.

The roses blush when I start to rhyme,
Puns fall flat, but I think it's fine.
A joke about weeds makes them uproar,
The laughter echoes, oh, give me more!

So here I stand, a poet confused,
In worlds of rhymes, hilariously amused.
With heartstrings tied to the roots below,
My silly verses put on a show!

The Nature of Reflection in Reeds

Down by the river, the reeds dance and sway,
Reflecting silly thoughts in a playful way.
I try to rhyme with a frog on a log,
But he croaks a tune, making me a cog.

The ducks sit gossiping, quacking away,
While I write puns that lead me astray.
A fish jumps high, a comical sight,
I lose my lines, but I'm feeling alright.

The ripples giggle as I ponder deep,
My words bobbing along like a sleepy sheep.
Nature's laughter tickles my mind,
Where deep reflections are hard to find.

In the reeds I find my jester's place,
With silly lines and a beaming face.
The river whispers secrets so bold,
That every writer wishes to behold!

Ode to the Wildflower Verse

Oh wildflowers, sprightly and free,
You bloom and tumble, what glee do we see!
Petals like laughter, colors so bright,
They tease my rhymes with sheer delight.

The bees buzz by, they listen and grin,
They hum my verses, oh, let the show begin!
With honey-dripped lines that stick to my feet,
I race through the fields, oh, what a treat!

In a daisy chain, I tie up my woes,
While a poppy laughs at my clumsy prose.
I crown myself king of this floral spree,
Declaring a holiday, just wait and see!

So here's to the wild, where nonsense takes flight,
With cheeky little poems, in sunshine so bright.
Let's dance with the blooms, and sing out of tune,
In this quirky garden, I'll howl at the moon!

Tales from the Whispering Wilderness

In the woods where the trees like to chat,
I write down tales of a curious cat.
He struts through the pines, with a swagger so bold,
Trading tall stories that never get old.

The squirrels gather, their chatter is rife,
As I pen down twists of their woodland life.
They flip-flop through branches, a real comedy,
Each leap and each bound, a wild symphony.

Beneath leafy crowns where the shadows peek,
A raccoon plays tricks, oh what a cheek!
With a wink and a nod, he steals every scene,
In this woodland theater, where laughs are routine.

So here's to the whispers that tickle the air,
With tales of the wild, my heart's laid bare.
In the wilderness' grasp, under the stars' gleam,
I dance with the humor that fuels every dream!

Echoes in the Meadow of Verse

In fields where oddities dance and prance,
The words weave tales that make us glance.
A cow in a hat, strumming a tune,
Leaves us giggling beneath the moon.

With each silly rhyme, a chuckle we find,
As daisies whisper secrets, oh so kind.
A goat tells a joke, we roll on the floor,
In the meadow of verse, there's always more.

Blossoms in every color, a cacophony bright,
They jest as they bloom, what a marvelous sight!
A frog croaks advice, in a comical spin,
In this humorous land, every laugh's a win.

So skip through the flowers, let laughter unfold,
In this meadow of echoes, let joy be bold.
With stanzas that frolic, let puns be our guide,
Here we dance with delight, so come, join the ride!

The Flourishing Grove of Ideas

In a grove where the thoughts like to tumble and twist,
A squirrel debates whether nuts can coexist.
The trees giggle softly, their branches all sway,
As ideas collide in a whimsical fray.

A rabbit writes sonnets with carrots as quills,
While fireflies flicker, lighting up all the thrills.
'What rhymes with orange?' the owl gives a hoot,
In this thriving retreat, creativity's astute.

With mushrooms as chairs, we sit and we dream,
In a world where the nonsense is part of the theme.
The wisdom we gather, both quirky and bright,
Turns the ordinary into a dazzling sight.

So relish the laughter, let ideas take flight,
In this flourishing grove, every mind's a delight.
With whimsy and wonder, we'll craft the absurd,
In a realm of surprises, where joy's never blurred!

Swaying Grasses of Inspiration

Through grasses that sway, the giggles arise,
With each tickle and tease, they paint the skies.
A worm writes a novel, penning it slow,
While butterflies whisper secrets in tow.

The breeze carries chuckles, a ticklish breeze,
As daisies throw parties, with snacks to appease.
A chicken who dances, causing quite a stir,
In this land of delight, who would dare to deter?

The chubby old hedgehog, with wisdom to share,
Tells tales of mischief, with flair and with care.
The ants hold a meeting, debating their plans,
To march in a line, while forming small bands.

So sway through this meadow, where laughter's the prize,

Find joy in the simple, beneath vast, funny skies.
Inspiration is found in the quirkiest seams,
As life spins a yarn, full of whimsical dreams!

Harvesting Thoughts from the Earth

In fields where the thoughts grow wild and free,
 We pluck up ideas like ripe fruit from a tree.
 A scarecrow recites poems, quite out of tune,
While crows share a giggle, the sun's rising soon.

The carrots all chuckle, their tops in a flurry,
 As brussels sprouts gossip, no need to hurry.
 'The corn's in on the joke!' a beetroot will shout,
In this patch of odd humor, there's always a route.

With harvest baskets filled with wit and delight,
 We gather up laughter, our spirits take flight.
 As pumpkins juggle thoughts, round and absurd,
 We revel in the whimsy, every line, every word.

So come to our garden, where nonsense takes root,
 In this bounty of laughter, there's always a hoot.
 With smiles in abundance, all tangled in mirth,
 We're harvesting joy from the depths of the earth!

Aria of the Evergreen Heart

In a park where the squirrels dance,
They jest and they prance, with a nut-sorting glance.
The daisies hold meetings, quite serious indeed,
Discussing the weather, and who takes the lead.

The breeze has a chuckle, it tickles the trees,
The robins compose songs, a symphonic tease.
While daisies gossip, and tulips start to jest,
Even the weeds think they're surely the best.

A worm wrote a poem, but forgot how to rhyme,
He curled up in laughter, said, "Maybe next time!"
The flowers roll petals, all laughing with glee,
In this merry garden, how funny it be!

So join in the chorus, take heed of the cheer,
Nature's absurdities surely endear.
For laughter's the sunlight that helps us all grow,
In this verdant domain, our hearts overflow.

A Tidal Wave of Verdant Whispers

The grass whispers secrets to the passing breeze,
While daisies conspire, under bumblebee tease.
A leaf once declared, with a fluttering shout,
'Let's start a parade! Who's in? Raise your sprout!'

The tulips wore hats, made of petals and sun,
They pranced around proudly, declaring their fun.
With each gust of laughter, they spun in delight,
While daisies debated who'd dance through the night.

A gopher chimed in, with a top hat and tail,
His puns about carrots were surely to regale.
They giggled at shadows, and sighed with mirth,
In this riot of color, they found their worth.

So remember, dear reader, as life rolls and sways,
Nature's a comedian, in wonderful ways.
There's joy in the garden, and fun in the green,
A tidal wave of laughter, wherever you lean!

Echoes of a Leafy Narrative

Once a leaf on a branch, thought it'd be a star,
So it wrote up a script, but it didn't go far.
With birds as the critics, and clouds as the crew,
They laughed at the plot, said the story won't do.

The sun overheard and let out a roar,
He said, "Dear leaf, let's not settle the score!"
The raindrops all giggled, with glee as they fell,
For writing in nature's just like a broadwell.

The flowers prattled on about petals they wore,
In their flowery debates, went boldly for more.
Their nectar discussions, quite sweet on the breeze,
Tickled the air with their fragrant unease.

So here in this thicket, where stories abound,
The echoes of laughter are life all around.
With each little whisper that rustles the tale,
Nature's a comedian, we'll all laugh and sail!

The Palette of Nature's Breath

In a meadow of colors, where daisies unite,
Brush strokes of laughter paint day into night.
The sunflowers giggle, exchanged sunny sights,
While clouds threw confetti in soft, frothy flights.

The grass sways in rhythm, a dance quite absurd,
As critters debate who has the best word.
A worm wrote a joke about compost and weeds,
It had all of the blossoms in fits of loud heaves.

The peacock was strutting, but tripped on a leaf,
He squawked, oh so loudly, proclaiming his grief.
While butterflies laughed, they took flight and spun,
Even dandelions got in on the fun.

So paint your own canvas, with humor and sass,
In the palette of nature, let laughter amass.
For joy is the pigment that bursts into view,
In this vibrant collection, there's always room for you!

www.ingramcontent.com/pod-product-compliance
Lightning Source LLC
Chambersburg PA
CBHW071815160426
43209CB00003B/97